CREEPY, KOOKY SCIENCE

Long-Lost Civilizations

Joyce Goldenstern

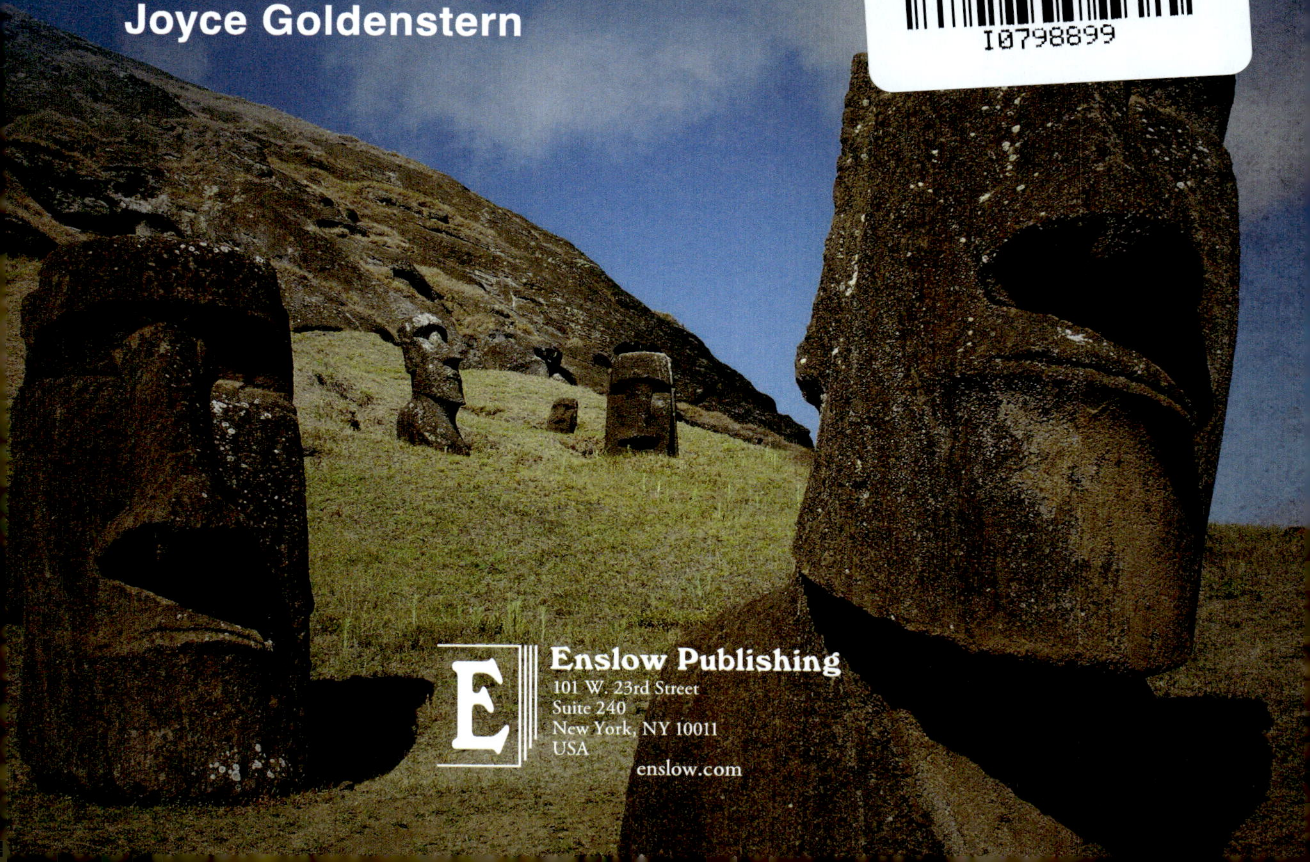

Enslow Publishing
101 W. 23rd Street
Suite 240
New York, NY 10011
USA
enslow.com

Published in 2019 by Enslow Publishing, LLC.
101 W. 23rd Street, Suite 240, New York, NY 10011

Cataloging-in-Publication Data

Names: Goldenstern, Joyce.
Title: Long-lost civilizations / Joyce Goldenstern.
Description: New York : Enslow Publishing, 2019. | Series: Creepy, kooky science | Audience: Grades 5-8. | Includes bibliographic references and index.
Identifiers: ISBN 9781978504516 (library bound) | ISBN 9781978505520 (pbk.)
Subjects: LCSH: Extinct cities—Juvenile literature. | Archaeology—History—Juvenile literature. | Civilization, Ancient—Juvenile literature.
Classification: LCC CC176.G65 2019 | DDC 930.1—dc23

Printed in the United States of America

To Our Readers: We have done our best to make sure all websites in this book were active and appropriate when we went to press. However, the author and the publisher have no control over and assume no liability for the material available on those websites or on any websites they may link to. Any comments or suggestions can be sent by email to customerservice@enslow.com.

Portions of this book originally appeared in *Lost Cities*.

Photo Credits: Cover, p. 1 niall dunne/Shutterstock.com; p. 6 Louis Jean Desprez/Getty Images; p. 8 Peter Langer/Perspectives/Getty Images; p. 11 Patrick Gijsbers/Shutterstock.com; p. 14 Maria Swärd/Moment/Getty Images; p. 17 Heritage Images/Hulton Fine Art Collection/Getty Images; p. 19 G. Dagli Orti/De Agostini Picture Library/Getty Images; p. 21 Rischgitz/Hulton Archive/Getty Images; p. 23 Iryna Savina/Shutterstock.com; p. 25 Werner Forman/Universal Images Group/Getty Images; p. 27 buteo/Shutterstock.com; p. 31 Private Collection/© Look and Learn/Bridgeman Images; p. 32 DEA/A. Dagli Orti/De Agostini Picture Library/Getty Images; p. 35 suronin/Shutterstock.com; p. 38 Avis De Miranda/Shutterstock.com; p. 40 BlackMac/Shutterstock.com.

Contents

Introduction

"Long lost civilizations." The words conjure mysteries and an invitation to investigate those mysteries. This book will uncover secrets of five "long-lost civilizations."

Bonampak in Mexico

Bloody and warlike images on the dyed walls of the city—what do they mean? This question frames the mystery of Bonampak, a Maya settlement in Chiapas, Mexico. Previously, most experts had thought the Maya lived a peaceful life, centered around culture and religion. The discovery in the 1940s of the murals at Bonampak changed that understanding. The images on the walls include aggressive raids, bloodletting, and torture. How could such cruelty suddenly infect a tranquil society? And did such a change signal the demise of a civilization?

Troy in Turkey

According to mythology, Paris of Troy sailed the Aegean Sea in search of Helen, the most beautiful woman in the world. He found her in Sparta, Greece, and fell hopelessly in love. Even though she was married to Menelaus, Paris brought her back home to Troy. Menelaus plotted revenge. Soon a thousand Greek warships headed toward Troy. Did Helen and Paris really exist? Did Greece and Troy actually fight a war—or were the war and the city of Troy only part of the legend?

Machu Picchu in Peru

A place so high up that clouds shroud its temples—from this remote site emerges an enigma. Why would the Inca of Peru build a settlement in such a difficult place? The Inca excelled at engineering and administration. They were good at building roads and bridges. Maybe constructing such a distant settlement proved less difficult for the Inca than it would have for a less-skilled people. One might also consider their high regard for astronomy, especially for the sun. Maybe the beautiful mountain location of Machu Picchu proved suitable for prayer and worship. Would archaeologists find clues to unlock the mysteries of Machu Picchu?

Mohenjo Daro and Harappa in the Indus Valley (Pakistan and India)

Who were the first people to settle the Indus Valley in India? For a long time, the Aryans claimed that achievement. And yet rumors lingered—hazy stories about fort-building settlers who inhabited

Mount Vesuvius erupted in 79 CE, destroying the Roman city of Pompeii.

the Indus Valley long before the Aryans moved in. Would archaeologists find relics of these forts? Would they be able to piece together what had happened to the people who built them?

Pompeii in Italy

Beneath ashes and stone, skeletons posed, caught in a moment of sudden death. A baby cradled in the arms of its mother. A young woman crying with her face in a pillow. A family huddled together, braced against oncoming hot mud and gas. The volcano in the mountain Vesuvius in 79 CE had been recorded. But Pompeii, the city it had destroyed, lay long buried. Pompeii held secrets about everyday life in ancient Rome. Would archaeologists figure out the stories from artifacts? How would scientists explain the hapless victims? Why had they been unable to escape their doom?

CHAPTER 1

Bonampak: A Painted Story of Warriors

According to Mayan mythology, humans once not only could look to the past. They could, like the gods, see into the future. However, as humans craved power, the gods took this gift from them. Humans could no longer see ahead, only behind in time. Thus. the wall painters who painted a Mayan story at Bonampak could not see the tragedies of their future. They painted with confidence. They painted with bright colors and an abundance of detail. They painted a story of victory in war and strength in the kingdom. They did not realize that the ending of their rule and their culture loomed just ahead. In the language of the Maya, *Bonampak* means "dyed walls." The wall painters did not realize that the lavish murals they painted would never be fully completed.[1]

Scouts Show the Way

Many writers have called Bonampak a lost city, but to the Lacandn Indians who live in Chiapas, Bonampak was not a lost city at all. The Lacandn, descendants of the Maya, sometimes visited the ruins of their ancestors. From time to time, they would chop away weeds on the overgrown trails to return to this sacred spot, but

In 1946, Mayan descendants led documentarian Giles Healey to Bonampak, where he saw structures such as these.

even for the Lacandn, the significance of the city with its magnificent murals had been lost. More than a thousand years had passed since Mayan artists painted the murals in about 800 CE. The Lacandn spoke a different language from that of their forebears; their customs had changed. What story did the city have to tell? Not even the Lacandn could say. Aside from the Lacandn, no one in modern times knew about Bonampak. Then, in 1946, the United Fruit Company hired Giles Healey (1901–1980) to make a documentary film about Mayan ruins. Healey hoped to film as many sites as possible.[2] For a few months, he lived among the Lacandn, hoping to gain their confidence so that they would show him unexplored sites. Several Lacandn scouts agreed to lead Healey through the rain forest to Bonampak.

Murals Tell a Story

His first view of Bonampak did not impress Healey. Most of the structures stood in shambles; weeds and vines grew from crumbling walls. Healey began shooting photographs of sculptures and inscriptions. The guides had more to show him: hidden behind dense vegetation stood a temple with three rooms. Immense murals graced the walls of each room. The grime of centuries had dulled the colors of the murals, but later, when archaeologists smeared kerosene on the walls, magnificent colors were uncovered: blue sky over battle scenes, red pigment in indoor scenes, green swirls outlined in red suggesting vegetation, and white-clothed figures. More impressive than the color, though, were the lines and form of the murals. The balanced compositions drew the viewer's eye to dramatic action scenes. The murals in each room told part of what seemed to be one entire story. In the first room, men disguised themselves as animal gods. One wore a pointed snout, another dressed as an alligator, and a third threatened others with a huge crab claw. In another panel, women observed attendants dressing a royal chief in an elaborate jaguar skin. Twelve musicians nearby prepared for some type of ceremony in preparation for a battle. Five musicians shook rattles, one beat a drum, three struck tortoise shells with antlers, one blew a whistle, and two sounded trumpets.

Going on a Dig

Someday you may have the chance to join an archaeological dig. If so, you will have to plan ahead. You will attend a meeting to learn about the purpose of the dig. You will be told what equipment to bring and what skills you will use. You will learn where you will sleep and eat.[3] Karl Ruppert was an anthropologist who studied Bonampak. His planning advice to others included information about the lack of water at the site and the swampy trails into the site. He said everyone would need to hunt for food: deer, birds, and wild pigs.[4]

Blood Prints Mark the Wall

The action continued in the second room, where a raid was in progress. Painted warriors dressed in costumes and jewelry were attacking a village

This red handprint is from the Uxmal site in Mexico. Mayan muralists marked painted walls with handprints, possibly as a sign of completion.

in what seemed to be a surprise raid. Their victims had no weapons and were easily captured by spear-wielding warriors, one of whom dragged a prisoner away by his hair. In another part of the mural, prisoners pricked and cut their fingers and hands. What did this bloodletting signify? Some anthropologists thought it had to do with the Mayan custom of leaving handprints on walls. The prisoners may have been preparing to leave their marks in blood. The Lacandn still believed in recent times that red handprints on a building were a sign of completion.[5] Other anthropologists wondered if the bloodletting signaled something more sinister, the forthcoming human sacrifice. In the third room, the warriors celebrated their victory with a dance and sacrificial ceremony. Again the musicians sounded their instruments. The body of a dead enemy soldier was sprawled out on some steps. Presumably he had just been sacrificed; a captor held a vessel with human blood and a heart in it. The blood was to be smeared on an idol.[6]

Scientists Figure Out Clues

Anthropologists try to figure out what such scenes reveal about life in ancient times. Cultural anthropologists study customs, like the Maya and Lacandn custom of leaving handprints. They can help interpret the ceremonies shown in art. Physical anthropologists study bones and physical artifacts; they know how to determine the composition and the age of paint used in murals. Archaeologists uncover ruins, then study and preserve them.

At Bonampak, it was an archaeologist who knew that kerosene would help bring out the color of the murals without ruining them. These scientists worked together to interpret the Bonampak discoveries. Never before had such details of Mayan life been seen. Most Mayan art uses symbols to depict gods and religious signs, but the murals of Bonampak are very realistic, with abundant details. One scholar described "noble young men" dancing, "wearing towering headdresses" and women "white-robed . . . seated on thrones, [drawing] blood from their tongues."[7]

The Maya Turn to War

The murals at Bonampak changed scholarly opinion about the Maya. For example, some historians previously had thought of the Maya as totally peaceful people. They had contrasted the peaceful Maya with the warrior Aztecs, a Mexican civilization that sacrificed human beings to the gods. Why had historians and anthropologists thought that the Maya were peaceful? Partly because Mayan sculpture does not show battle scenes. The murals at Bonampak, however, indicate that around 800 CE, the Maya engaged in raids and surprise attacks. They also show that human sacrifice may have taken place. The murals also changed beliefs about the role of women in Mayan society. The murals show many women observing and even participating in ceremonies. Cultural anthropologists previously had thought that women played no role in Mayan religious ceremonies. Why had they thought this? Anthropologists had observed that modern Lacandn women avoided religious sites. The anthropologists assumed that this also had occurred in classical Mayan times. Now since the discovery of the Bonampak murals, many anthropologists think that women may once have enjoyed many rights in Mayan civilization but later

Many of the murals at Bonampak tell stories of raids and attacks as well as human sacrifice, challenging an understanding of the Maya as a peaceful people.

lost them. Perhaps as the society paid more tribute to male warriors, it began to find women less valuable.[8]

A military spirit might have signaled the end of the Mayan civilization, which had flourished for about six hundred years. The Maya had developed a calendar and a writing system. They created beautiful temples and sculptures. Did the Maya then suddenly begin to change? Did they start to think more about war and less about culture? No one knows for sure. But their civilization did begin to crumble soon after artists painted the battle scenes on the walls at Bonampak. The murals themselves were never completely finished, as the inhabitants of Bonampak mysteriously began to abandon the settlement.

CHAPTER 2

Troy: More than a Legend?

"Sing, O goddess," begins the *Iliad* (or at least Samuel Butler's 1898 translation of that ancient poem). The first character to speak is the priest Chryses, who says, "[M]ay the gods who dwell in Olympus grant you to sack the city of Priam, and to reach your homes in safety." The city of Priam was the legendary city of Troy. Chryses is addressing the Greeks, whose war against the Trojans is the subject of many stories, of which the *Iliad* is the best known. (Ilium was another name for Troy.)

The poet Homer probably composed the *Iliad* in about 762 BCE. But long before that, legends existed about Troy. These legends were part of an oral tradition. The Trojan War supposedly took place in the twelfth or thirteenth century BCE. Thanks to many oral storytellers, information about the war got passed down before it was finally written as a book. But was the information accurate? Modern people tend to distrust the oral tradition. They think that through the generations, inaccuracies slip into the accounts or certain facts are forgotten.[1] They also note that ancient religious beliefs or myths are added. Thus, before the 1880s, many scholars thought the Trojan War and "the long-lost civilization" of Troy were simply legends and not rooted in historical fact.

Paris's Folly

According to a myth, here is how the war began. Hera, the jealous queen of Olympia; Athena, the goddess of wisdom; and Aphrodite, the goddess of love, argued one day about their beauty. As they quibbled back and forth, they walked together down the slope of Mount Ida. Suddenly they came upon Paris, son of Priam, the king of Troy. Paris was disguised as a shepherd. Each goddess tried to win favor with the shepherd, hoping he would choose her as the most beautiful. In the end he chose Aphrodite. Her promise to give him a beautiful bride in exchange for his vote intrigued Paris. Soon Paris set sail on the Aegean Sea, seeking trade and adventure, and looking for his bride. He heard stories of a Greek woman named Helen, said to be the most beautiful in the world. When Paris sailed to Sparta, he found Helen. Indeed she was lovely! He fell hopelessly in love. However, she was already married to

King Menelaus. Nonetheless, Paris courted Helen and brought her with him back to Troy. King Menelaus plotted revenge. Soon a thousand Greek warships headed toward Troy. Helen became known as a face that launched a thousand ships. Much of this story does not seem rooted in historical fact. The jealousy of goddesses, Paris's disguise, Helen's treacherous beauty—these seem fanciful. But did Greek and Trojan soldiers really wage a war? Thanks to the work of archaeologists in the nineteenth century, this question has been answered. Today many scholars do believe that Greece and Troy fought a long war. Three thousand years ago, both cities traded on the Aegean Sea, and both wanted control of the sea. Their economic rivalry may have led to war.

According to Greek mythology, the beauty of Helen of Troy outshone that of all other mortal women.

An Archaeologist's Imagination

Scholars believe that the legend of Troy may be based in fact, partly because of the work of Heinrich Schliemann, an archaeologist who was born in Germany in 1822. Troy sparked Schliemann's imagination early in his life. He refused to believe that the heroes had not really existed. And he was disappointed when his father told him that Troy had been completely destroyed.[2]

Schliemann, who grew up to be an extremely successful businessman, decided to use his money to follow his dream and search for Troy. In 1868, he toured Greece for a few weeks, then he took off across the Aegean Sea toward Turkey. First Schliemann investigated Burnarbashi, which was 10 miles (16 kilometers) from the Aegean Sea. He imagined Troy as a gleaming city with white marble buildings and majestic gates, but at Burnarbashi, he found a rubbish heap. Homer had described Troy as being near the seashore, so Schliemann decided to investigate the site at Hissarlik. Schliemann wanted to begin digging at the site, which included a hill and a plain below, like those described in the *Iliad*. His companions urged him not to be too hasty; it would be best to begin in the spring when the weather was better. Also, to dig he needed permission from the Turkish government.

Archaeology's Beginnings

In the late 1800s, archaeology was a new science. For centuries, people had collected ancient artifacts for their own pleasure. Archaeologists, however, were interested in learning from artifacts. Artifacts are human-made objects that can be moved about without changing their appearance. (A vase is an artifact, for example, but a bridge is not.) Features are human-made objects that are difficult to move about. These would include bridges, campfire remains, and trash pits. In addition to features and artifacts, small bits of bone, shell, and charcoal help archaeologists to date and classify their finds.

Hissarlik Hill in Turkey is believed to be the site of Homeric Troy. Shown here are the walls and gate of the city.

Archaeologists started to think about the ethics of their profession. Today it would be considered unethical for an archaeologist to keep artifacts for profit. Archaeologists respect the rights of the countries where they work. They believe that artifacts should be used to help all people know about the past, so their finds usually are displayed in museums or are given to universities for study. Schliemann wanted to be part of the new science of archaeology, but at the same time, he longed to find buried treasure for his own profit. He returned to Hissarlik in the spring of 1870 and began to dig. He found many artifacts: broken pieces of pottery, coins, lance heads of green stone, and boars tusks. These appeared to him to be very primitive, and they seemed to be older than the time of the Trojan War, which historians thought took place around 1200 BCE.

Archaeological Records

At first, Schliemann was not careful to record information about his discoveries, but he listened eagerly to the advice of scientists, who told him that he must keep a journal. He must record the date and time of each discovery and the exact location where he unearthed each article. One scientist warned him, "You must take care to report these things accurately. Or else you will never be able to come to definite conclusions on your wonderful discoveries."[4]

Heeding all of this advice, Schliemann became more scientific in his approach. He discovered that nine separate cities had been built at Hissarlik. Some were older than Troy, one perhaps from 3000 BCE. Some

What Is the Difference Between a Historian and an Archaeologist?

A historian usually studies documents to understand the past. For example, a historian of the US Civil War may read letters soldiers wrote back home from the battlefront in order to understand the daily hardships of the military. An archaeologist, on the other hand, studies material culture or "things" to understand the past.[3] He or she may dig up a battlefield or military camp to look for bullets or utensils or keepsakes. From these, an archaeologist may try to interpret the battle plans of generals or the sentiments of soldiers.

were more recent, the most recent possibly from 300 BCE. Schliemann, confident that one of the nine cities surely was the Troy of legends, named his findings according to legend. He named one immense wall after the goddess Athena; he named a statue of a woman after Helen of Troy. When he found a broken chest with silver vases, he named it Priam's treasure. His adventures sparked an interest in ordinary people. The public supported and followed the work of archaeologists who continued Schiemann's work. These archaeologists dated and classified more artifacts. Like Schiemann, some archaeologists today believe that one of the nine cities at Hissarlik truly is the legendary Troy.

Schliemann whimsically called some of the artifacts he found Priam's treasure after the imagined wealth of the Trojan king.

CHAPTER 3

Machu Picchu: Beauty and Mystery

"Surprise followed surprise until there came the realization that we were in the midst of as wonderful ruins as ever found in Peru. It seemed almost incredible that this city, only five days' journey from Cuzco, should have remained so long undescribed and comparatively unknown."[1] With these words, explorer Hiram Bingham (1875–1956) remembered his first visit to Machu Picchu in 1911.

A Surprise in the Andes

The Inca had ruled in the Andes Mountains from about 1430 to 1532 CE. Hiram Bingham, with an expedition organized by Yale

Machu Picchu, an Inca citadel, stands high in the mountains in a remote area of Peru.

University, had come to Peru hoping to find Inca ceremonial sites. A local farmer had encouraged Bingham to seek ruins on a mountain ridge called Machu Picchu. To get there, Bingham, who was not in good physical shape, first crossed rapids of a roaring river. A rickety bridge of some logs tied together with vines offered the only way across. Bingham wrote that no one could survive the icy cold rapids. Those who fell in would immediately be dashed to pieces against the rocks.[2] Bingham got down on his stomach to crawl slowly across the bridge, creeping along 6 inches (15 centimeters) at a time.[3]

A guide led Bingham to beautifully constructed stone-faced terraces.[4] Bingham marveled at a curved temple and other structures. Most amazing was the stonework. With great artistic ability, the Incas had cut stones into fine geometrical shapes, each stone fitting perfectly together with another without any glue or mortar between them. Bingham could not even slip the slender blade of a knife through the stone fittings. The stones might have grown together, Bingham wrote.[5]

Clues in the Ruins

Bingham wanted to identify the ruins, but jungle growth covered many of them. Bingham wrote that "massive trees, two feet thick [61 cm], perched on the gable ends of small . . . houses."[6] Workers helped him chop away the jungle plants that hid the structures. The city that emerged amazed him. He tried to guess the use of each building; he wrote and spoke about his find. Soon other archaeologists arrived and gradually a story about the Inca unfolded.

A lost site cannot tell a complete story, but it can offer hints and clues. The Inca had no written language. Officials kept records with *quipa*, a system of counting that used knots on a cord. The knots are evidence of the Inca accounting system, but they do not tell us a lot about daily life. By looking at ruins, archaeologists can tell more about the Inca: they built roads, and they mastered stone architecture. They ruled an empire that extended north and south from Ecuador to Chile, stretching 2,500 miles (4,023 km). Such accomplishments require a lot of organization. Strong leaders must have exercised great power over lowly workers who carried the stones needed to build the temples and walls and roads.

Quipa helped officials keep track of such things as the numbers of llamas and quantities of produce they had.

When archaeologists investigated the ruins of Machu Picchu, they learned even more. They found many temples and shrines, more than had been found in most Inca cities. Bingham liked to brag that Machu Picchu was the original, mythological home of Inca ancestors. Most archaeologists disagreed with him because none of the buildings showed evidence of the simple early Inca style. They thought that the Inca probably built the buildings at the site in the 1500s, at the peak of their power. Machu Picchu may have been a royal estate or vacation home, belonging to a ruler and his kin. Farmers would have worked for the estate, planting crops in the soil of terraces.[7] Farming is difficult in high, rocky mountains. The stone terraces built by the Inca probably helped to level the land for farming. Servants and caretakers would have populated the town. The many religious temples and shrines attested to religious rituals important to the royal court.[8]

More Clues in the Midst

Some Incan descendants continue practicing what they say are old ways, and it is possible that some of their customs are similar to customs of the ancient Inca. For example, the descendants still live in the highland mountains, farming and weaving in a traditional manner. Geography and climate are also helpful for understanding daily life in the past. The exquisite beauty of the high mountains at Machu Picchu may have inspired religious feelings and led to the building of places of worship.

Stone Pinnacle on a Ridge

One mysterious structure at Machu Picchu baffled scientists. They eventually named the structure Intihuatana. In the language of the

The Intihuatana stone was a kind of solar clock or calendar to mark the winter solstice and other important times of the year.

Inca, this means hitching post to the sun. (A hitching post is a place to tie up a riding animal.) The Inca did not ride horses; they used llamas and alpacas, which easily climb up steep mountains. The Inca sometimes tied them to hitching posts. But how could anyone tie up the sun? The path to Intihuatana passes a large chamber, called the Ornamental Chamber. Bingham guessed that the Inca displayed their dead in this chamber. He knew that explorers had found mummies in similar chambers in other parts of Peru. From Spanish writings, it is known that the Inca mummified royal leaders when they died. They displayed them in rooms and even carried them in parades as a sign of respect to their lasting power. Above the Ornamental Chamber there are several terraces to climb. At the peak of a mountain ridge above the terraces is an impressive stone pinnacle, a point that rises 6 feet (about 2 meters) above a massive granite altar. One traveler wrote that the sun might appear to be tied up there for a moment. He said, "In his [the sun's] passage through his zenith, he might sit down in all his glory."[9]

This guess about the pinnacle made sense to archaeologists. It added to other information they had about the Inca's regard for the sun. One Spanish writer had noted that the Inca practiced astronomy, observing the movements of the sun in order to predict the best time to plant crops. "They calculated the month, day, hour and precise moment for sowing their crops."[10]

The Inca Road

Archaeologists continue to investigate Machu Picchu. In the 1990s, they uncovered "the Inca Road" in Machu Picchu. The Inca Road was important economically as well as religiously to Machu Picchu. The road ended at the Urubamba River, so it helped in the transportation of goods. By connecting Machu Picchu to river traffic, the road served an economic function. The road also connected the center of Machu Picchu to surrounding cemeteries. People could march in procession down the road as they buried the dead. Thus, the road also had a ceremonial or religious function.[11]

The Sun in Incan Religion

The sun was also important in the religion of the Inca. They worshiped the sun at a festival twice each year. A Spanish priest described this festival: "The rulers dressed in magnificent robes; they wore headdresses of gold and silver. Awnings of beautiful feathers lined the avenues. As soon as the sunrise began, they started to chant in marvelous harmony . . . While chanting, each of them shook his foot."[12] As the sun rose, the chanting got louder and louder. After the sunrise, young girls brought corn beer in pitchers. They also offered bales of coca to the sun. Everyone thanked the sun for past harvests, praying for future crops. As the day closed, the chanting began again, this time sounding to the Spanish priest like a sad murmur. As the sun sank in the sky, the voices died away. The voices of Machu Picchu died away as well. After the Spaniards defeated the Inca in 1532, Inca civilization crumbled. No one knows for sure exactly when people deserted Machu Picchu or where they went. They probably settled in less remote areas in the mountains and farmed. Now shadows fall on the abandoned city, but so does the sun. For a moment each day it seems to stop, tied to a hitching post.

CHAPTER 4

Indus Civilization: Questions Answered and Unanswered

Its language captured in script has never been deciphered. One of its chief rivers, Saraswati, has disappeared; it has completely dried up. Its expected palaces and temples do not exist and probably never did exist. Goods that its traders brought home remain unknown. After thriving almost one thousand years, its cities suddenly collapsed. And yet the discovery and excavation in the 1920s of Harappa and Mohenjo Daro took "Europe by storm."[1] These cities were two of the most important cities of the newly discovered Indus civilization. Urban dwellings with indoor bathrooms and excellent sewers impressed the

West. Comfortable houses on "well laid-out streets" invited favorable comment. Seals "bearing an enigmatic script" fascinated Europeans.[2]

This artwork depicts life in the Indus Valley. Harappa and Mohenjo Daro, two cities known for their industry and crafts, were part of the Indus civilization.

The Indus civilization had flourished in the Indus Valley from about 2500 BCE to about 1500 BCE. Harappa and Mohenjo Daro first cradled civilization on the Indian subcontinent. The two cities had prospered for nearly a thousand years. Commerce and river trade helped support them, but they drew their greatest wealth from agriculture. Wheat, barley, dates, field peas, and even cotton thrived on the fertile soil of the Indus River Valley. Mohenjo Daro lay near the Indus River in what today is Pakistan. Harappa lay about 400 miles (644 km) northeast on the Ravi River, a tributary of the mighty Indus.

Toolmakers and Artisans

The wealth from agriculture supported many crafts. Toolmakers crafted chisels, axes, knives, and other tools from bronze and

These terracotta figurines were found in Mohenjo Daro. Some artisans of the Indus Valley excelled at making imaginative toys for children.

copper. Potters used wheels to make pots and then painted them with red ochre. Weavers wove cotton into garments. Some artisans must have even known how to create statues using molds. Among the ruins, archaeologists found a statue of a pert and pretty dancer cast in bronze. The inhabitants had had leisure time. They threw dice and played board games. They made toys for their children: little birds and tiny carts with wheels, miniatures of real oxcarts that adults used for plowing. The people of these river cities evidently had a strong sense of ownership.

Archaeologists found hundreds of seals, used for marking belongings and decorated with sunken patterns of animals, such as elephants, rhinoceroses, antelopes, crocodiles, and even unicorns. Most impressively, though, inscriptions marked each seal. Perhaps the inscriptions were personal names. No one knows for sure because no one has been able to decipher them. Nonetheless, the inscriptions show that the people of the Indus Valley had developed writing. About 1500 BCE, Aryans invaded the Indian subcontinent, and everything started to change.

Invasion and Destruction

Until the 1920s, no one in modern times knew about the people of Mohenjo Daro and Harappa. Both cities lay buried and forgotten. It was thought that the warrior Aryans were the first to bring civilization to the Indus Valley. The Aryans, it was thought, had found wandering tribes when they arrived. Yet some scholars wondered: in the Aryan saga RigVeda, there were references to forts. Indra, chief god of the Aryans, was called Purmamdara, which means "fort destroyer."[3] One passage described Indra destroying ninety forts; in another passage, Indra rends forts as age consumes a garment. Scholars wondered whether this meant that the conquering Aryans had found a settled civilization, rather than a nomadic people.

Excavation and Discovery

In the 1920s, the Indian Archaeological Survey excavated many sites in the Indus Valley. It was during these excavations that archaeologists unearthed the cities: first Harappa, and then Mohenjo Daro.

Harappa, a city about 3 miles (5 km) in circumference, stood on a huge mound. Its most remarkable structure, a citadel about 460 yards (421 m) long and 215 yards (197 m) wide, rose high above the city. Bastions projected above the fort, a mighty baked brick wall surrounded it, and gates prevented enemies from entering. To the north of the fort stood huge granaries. Straight streets ran in a perfect grid. On the streets, modest but spacious houses once stood. They contained bathrooms and latrines. The city had excellent sewer and drainage systems. Mohenjo Daro, just like its sister city, boasted a towering citadel and huge granaries. The plan of the city followed a design similar to that of Harappa. Sewers and drainage systems were evident. Most impressive was a huge public bath, made watertight with baked bricks. Archaeologists found these structures in even better condition than those at Harappa. The mystery of the forts mentioned in the RigVeda had evidently been solved.

Clean and Green

Some scholars point to ecology as a way to understand the fall of Harappa and Mohenjo Daro. On the other hand, the people of the Indus Valley had many "green" practices. For example, they collected and used rainwater for crops. Their city planners designed drainage systems to keep their cities clean and sanitary. Construction workers could harness solar energy in sun-dried bricks. Artisans made pottery and toys from natural materials such as mud and clay and made tools from wood, stone, and metal.[4]

Ecology and Raids

Archaeologists found skeletons with sword cuts to the skull during excavation. These skulls testify to many Aryan raids on the cities, but scholars do not hold the Aryans completely responsible for the decline of the ancient civilization. Many other factors may have caused its fall. Some anthropologists who specialize in environmental issues speculate that the ecology of the region may have been a factor. The rivers had been a source of wealth for the inhabitants, offering trade routes and soil fertile from flooding. But the rivers could also have contributed to problems. Some theorize that the inhabitants may have destroyed the forests surrounding the rivers. The Indus Valley people used huge quantities of charcoal for fuel in smelting copper.

The city of Mohenjo Daro serves as a model of city planning and design with its sewers, drainage systems, and citadel.

Some anthropologists reason that the inhabitants kept cutting down trees to manufacture charcoal. Wood from trees also fired some of the bricks used for construction. For about a thousand years, structures continually had to be mended and rebuilt. Old cities crumbled, and new ones were built on top of them. As trees were cut down, the bare hills no longer absorbed the water from heavy rains. The rainwater could rush down the hills to the swelling river, and even high dikes might fail. As the people struggled with floods, their resources and energy may have dwindled.[5] When Aryan invaders challenged them, the weakened inhabitants could not defend their magnificent cities.

CHAPTER 5

Pompeii and Herculaneum: Ashes, Stones, and Bones

"You could hear the shrieks of women, the wailing of infants, and the shouting of men; some were calling their parents, others their children or their wives, trying to recognize them by their voices. People bewailed their own fate or that of their relatives, and there were some who prayed for death in their terror of dying. Many besought the aid of the gods, but still more imagined there were no gods left, and that the universe was plunged into eternal darkness for evermore," recounted Pliny the Younger (61–112 CE).[1]

On August 25, 79 CE, doom sounded for Roman towns along the coast of the Bay of Naples. Many thought the world was coming to an end. People had lived for centuries under the shadow of a mountain called Vesuvius, but they had not realized that that mountain was really a volcano. Ash fell at the rate of 6 inches (15 cm) per hour, devouring the town of Pompeii. An avalanche surged through the town of Herculaneum; black winds raged. Those who had remained in their homes could no longer escape; they suffocated or were crushed as buildings toppled. Some were flung into the air by the powerful winds.

Pliny did not live in the shadow of the volcano, but he did live in a town across the bay. As the sky darkened, Pliny watched with his uncle, Pliny the Elder (23–79 CE), who sailed off to investigate. The uncle never returned home; dense fumes choked and killed him as he reached the opposite shore. Pliny the Younger described the events of that August with chilling detail in an account that has survived for nearly two thousand years. After Pliny's time, everyone assumed that the two towns had been totally destroyed.

Discovery and Plunder

In 1709, a laborer was digging a shaft in the Italian town of Ercolano, near Naples, when his shovel struck a layer of ancient white marble. The white marble turned out to be part of a Roman theater. Ercolano, as it happened, had been built on Herculaneum, and the theater had been buried for almost two thousand years. Word of the discovery spread, but it was only in 1748 that some other workmen digging by a canal found remains of Herculaneum's sister city. This time the workers struck

Hot mud preserved artifacts through carbonization. Vesuvius did not totally destroy the cities.

upon bronze and marble statues and an inscription marking the site as ancient Pompeii. Unfortunately, the rulers of Naples, who did not care very much about history, looted the theater, carting off slabs of marble and bronze statues.

Archaeology and Excavation

By 1860, when archaeology had become a recognized science, archaeologists began excavations of Herculaneum and Pompeii. They soon found that the volcano had buried the towns without completely destroying them. Some of the mud from the volcano was extremely hot, carbonizing whatever it touched. Some of the mud was warm, preserving delicate items; even some of the food had not rotted away after two thousand years. Excavators found fruit in glass containers in the market and carbonized loaves of bread in a bakery shop oven. They also easily identified the skeletons of fish and sheep in a butcher shop. In one house, excavators found a table set for dinner. In the corner stood a pitcher for hot water and a brazier for cooking. On the wall, a sign warned about proper manners: *Don't put your dirty feet on our couch covers. If you bicker at the table, you'll have to go home. Be modest and don't make eyes at another man's wife.*[2]

Amusing signs and graffiti could be found throughout the towns. Love complaints were scribbled on walls along with bawdy jokes. There were signs advertising the price of wine, rent rates, and rewards for stolen property. Archaeologists found election slogans painted in red and black on many shop walls. Each trade—fishermen, dyers, bakers, and goldsmiths—urged citizens to vote for its candidate for mayor; one painted slogan even advertised the preferred candidate of street thieves![3]

The numerous election slogans testified to the strength of democracy in ancient Rome; graffiti suggested widespread literacy. One joker scribbled on a wall, "Everybody writes on the walls but me."[4] The ruins also revealed something about social class in ancient Rome. Fine jewelry, paintings, and statues revealed one side of life; taverns and obscene drawings showed another.

Sudden Death and Tragedy

Even today, parts of ancient Pompeii and Herculaneum remain buried. In 1982, scientists unearthed the scene of a heartbreaking tragedy in Herculaneum. The never before seen skeletons lay in beach chambers,

Telling the Difference

How does one tell a male skeleton from a female skeleton? Determining the sex from skeletal remains can be difficult. Sometimes with child skeletons, it is impossible. Most sex differences in bones are marked by puberty. A female skeleton will have a longer pubic bone than will a male skeleton. A long public bone helps women give birth with greater ease.[5] The teeth of men tend to be larger than those of women. Thus, teeth also help in identifying the sex of skeletons.[6]

Skeletons posed in defensive postures reveal the human tragedy of Pompeii and Herculaneum.

dressing rooms near the ocean. In one chamber, a family huddled together. A baby lay cradled in the arms of an adult. Another skeleton lay with its face to the ground, perhaps crying into a pillow.[7] From these skeletons, scientists have learned something about the volcano. The position and location of the skeletons suggest that these people met sudden death, that the hot mud and gas from the volcano rushed down the mountain at great speed. Scientists have observed such an event, called a glowing avalanche, after certain other volcanic eruptions. The skeletons showed that a glowing avalanche probably had occurred at Herculaneum.

Each skeleton had a story. One person lived the hard life of a slave; another had scars from battles. One wore expensive rings and bracelets. One died carrying her first child in her womb.[8] A boxer's bones showed healed injuries and the fracture of a rib and nose.[9] Yes, the dead could speak from the ashes of Vesuvius.

Chapter Notes

Chapter 1. Bonampak: A Painted Story of Warriors

1. Mary Miller and Claudia Brittenbam, *The Spectacle of the Late Maya Court: Reflections on the Murals of Bonampak* (Austin, TX.: University of Texas Press, 2013), p. 2.
2. Andre Emmerich, *Art Before Columbus* (New York, NY: Simon and Schuster, 1963), p. 139.
3. Joe Flatman, *Becoming an Archaeologist* (Cambridge, UK: Cambridge University Press, 2011), pp. 50–56.
4. Karl Ruppert. "Location, Environment, and History of the Site," in *Bonampak, Chiapas, Mexico* by Karl Ruppert, J. Eric S. Thompson, and Tatiana Proskouriakoff (Washington DC: Carnegie Institution, 1955), p. 8.
5. J. Eric S. Thompson, "The Subject Matter of the Murals," in Ruppert, Thompson, and Proskouriakoff, p. 8.
6. Ibid. p. 56.
7. Michael D. Coe and Stephen Houston, *The Maya, Ninth Edition* (New York, NY: Thames and Hudson, Inc., 2015), p. 150.
8. J. Eric S. Thompson, "Some Ethnological Notes on the Murals" in Ruppert, Thompson, and Proskouriakoff, p. 64.

Chapter 2. Troy: More than a Legend?

1. Susan Provost Beller, *The History Puzzle: How We Know What We Know About the Past* (Minneapolis, MN: Twenty-First Century Books, 2006), pp. 79–80.
2. This quotation is reported by Schliemann in his autobiography and reproduced in *Memoirs of Heinrich Schliemann: A Documentary Portrait*

Drawn from His Autobiographical Writings, Letters, and Excavation Reports by Leo Deuel (New York, NY: Harper & Row, 1977), p. 25.
3. Joe Flatman, *Becoming an Archaeologist* (Cambridge, UK: Cambridge University Press, 2011), p. 8.
4. Robert Payne, *The Gold of Troy* (New York, NY: Funk & Wagnalls, 1959), p. 155.

Chapter 3. Machu Picchu: Beauty and Mystery

1. Hiram Bingham, "Discovery of Machu Picchu" in *Machu Picchu: Unveiling the Mystery of the Incas,* ed. Richard L. Burger and Lucy C. Salazar (New Haven, CT: Yale University Press, 2004), p. 12.
2. Hiram Bingham, *Lost City of the Incas* (New York, NY: Atheneum, 1979), p. 149.
3. Ibid.
4. Bingham, p. 151.
5. Bingham, p. 153.
6. Quoted in John Hemming, *Machu Picchu* (New York, NY: Newsweek, 1981), p. 18.
7. Lucy C. Salazar. "Mysterious Royal Estate," in Burger and Salazar, p. 26.
8. Ibid.
9. George Squier, quoted in Hemming, p. 50.
10. Quoted in Hemming, p. 51.
11. Valencia Zegarra, "Recent Archaeological Investigations at Machu Picchu," in Burger and Salazar, pp. 79–81.
12. Quoted in Hemming, p. 51.

Chapter 4. Indus Civilization: Questions Answered and Unanswered

1. Jane R. McIntosh, *The Ancient Indus Valley: New Perspectives* (Santa Barbara, CA: ABC CLIO, 2008), pp. 4–6.

2. Ibid.
3. RigVeda quoted in *The Horizon Book of Lost Worlds,* ed. Marshall B. Davidson (New York, NY: American Heritage Publishing Company, 1962), p. 210.
4. Benita Sen, *Indus Valley: Green Lessons from the Past* (New Delhi, India: The Energy and Resources Institute, 2011), p. 30.
5. Bridget Allchin and Raymond Allchin, *The Rise of Civilization in India and Pakistan* (Cambridge, UK: Cambridge University Press, 1982), pp. 224–225; Davidson, p. 218; McIntosh pp. 23–24.

Chapter 5. Pompeii and Herculaneum: Ashes, Stones, and Bones

1. “The Destruction of Pompeii, 79 AD,” EyeWitness to History, 1999, http://www.eyewitnesstohistory.com/pompeii.htm.
2. Paul MacKendrick, *Mute Stones Speak* (New York, NY: W.W. Norton, 1983), p. 254.
3. MacKendrick, p. 249.
4. Helen H. Tanzer, *The Common People of Pompeii: A Study of the Graffiti* (Baltimore, MD: Johns Hopkins University Press, 1939), p. 6.
5. Estelle Lazer, *Resurrecting Pompeii* (New York, NY: Routledge, 2009), p. 120.
6. Lazer, p. 132.
7. Rick Gore, “The Dead Do Tell Tales at Vesuvius,” *National Geographic* (May 1984), pp. 557–614.
8. Ibid.
9. Lazer, p. 218.

Glossary

anthropologist A person who studies human origins and culture.

archaeology The study of the remains of past human cultures.

artisan A craftsperson; someone who makes things by hand.

BCE A system of dating that means "before the common era," or before the birth of Jesus Christ.

CE A system of dating that means "the common era." The birth of Jesus Christ serves as starting point of the common era.

ecology The study of the systems in nature and how they relate to one another.

excavation The digging up of something, for example, an ancient civilization.

feature A large, complex object showing human workmanship. A feature cannot be moved without being harmed or changed.

granary A storehouse where grain is kept.

legend A story that may be based in part on historical fact but that usually includes exaggeration or fiction.

material culture Objects of a civilization or culture as opposed to documents.

myth A religious story from an ancient religion that is no longer practiced, usually containing supernatural elements.

pinnacle The high point of a building or mountain.

seal A symbol or insignia stamped onto a document to show its official status or origin.

terrace A raised area, made for a road or planting, with the top leveled flat.

Important Dates

400,000 BCE Oldest evidence of human shelters.

25,000 BCE Cave paintings in Lascaux, France, and Altamira, Spain.

8000 BCE The first cities appear in Mesopotamia (modern Iraq) and Anatolia (modern Turkey).

3000 BCE Old Kingdom of Egypt rises; settlement of Troy; the Indus Valley civilization arises.

2700 BCE The first pyramids are built in Egypt.

2500 BCE The Indus Valley civilization begins to flourish.

1500 BCE The Indus Valley civilization is destroyed by Aryan invaders.

1200 BCE Destruction of Troy. Remains show the city was destroyed by fire and abandoned for four hundred years.

900–700 BCE The time during which Homer lived and composed the *Iliad*.

800 BCE First settlement of Pompeii by Oscans, an ancient people of Italy.

753 BCE The legendary date of the founding of Rome.

300 BCE Pompeii is conquered by Rome.

79 CE Mount Vesuvius erupts and destroys the Roman cities of Pompeii, Herculaneum, and Stabiae.

250 Classic Mayan civilization begins.

800 The walls of Bonampak are painted by Mayan artisans.

850 Bonampak is abandoned.

900 The end of Classic Mayan civilization.

1100–1200 Inca civilization begins.

1492 Columbus lands in the New World.

1532 Incas conquered by Spanish.

1748 Pompeii is rediscovered.

1870 Heinrich Schliemann begins excavations at Hissarlik, Turkey.

1911 Machu Picchu rediscovered by Hiram Bingham.

1922 Rediscovery of Mohenjo Daro.

1946 The Lacandn show the painted walls of Bonampak to Giles Healy.

Further Reading

Books

Bedell, J. M. *So, You Want to Work with the Ancient and Recent Dead?: Unearthing Careers from Paleontology to Forensic Science*. New York, NY: Aladdin, 2015.

Capek, Michael. *Unsolved Archaeological Mysteries*. North Mankato, MN: Capstone Press, 2016.

Huey, Lois M. *Children of the Past: Archaeology and the Lives of Kids*. Minneapolis, MN: Millbrook Press, 2017.

Meinking, Mary. *Machu Picchu: Digging Up the Past.* Minneapolis, MN: Essential Library, 2015.

Thompson, Clifford. *Archaeologists!* Broomall, PA: Mason Crest, 2016.

Websites

The British Museum Website on Life and Death: Pompeii and Herculaneum

www.britishmuseum.org/whats_on/exhibitions/pompeii_and_herculaneum.aspx

Read a detailed timeline of what happened each hour after Vesuvius erupted.

National Park Service, Archaeology Program

www.nps.gov/archeology/public/kids/kidsFour.htm#

Explore some fun activities for kids interested in archaeology.

Thought Company: Archaeology

www.thoughtco.com/archaeology-4133504

Read career information, as well as articles on many ancient civilizations.

Index